LEO:

A COMPLETE GUIDE TO THE LEO ASTROLOGY STAR SIGN

Sofia Visconti

Contents

INTRODUCTION

Astrology has fascinated humans for centuries. At its core it revolves around the notion that positions and motions of the planets and stars can influence and mirror our behavior, personality traits and life events. By analyzing the combination of placements at someone's birth moment astrologers, create birth charts (also known as natal charts) which serve as a guide to understanding an individual's character traits and life journey.

The zodiac plays an important role in astrology as it consists of twelve signs. Each sign falls within specific dates of the year. Each with their unique personality traits, strengths, weaknesses and distinct characteristics. In this book we provide an exploration of the Leo zodiac sign. The book has three objectives.

1. **Understanding**; We will delve deeply into the characteristics and traits that define Leos. Readers will gain an understanding of what makes individuals born under Leo unique. This includes exploring their strengths, weaknesses and how they navigate various aspects of life.

2. **Insights**; This book offers insights not only for Leo individuals but also for anyone interested in astrology. Through studying Leo readers can gain an understanding of astrology and how it can be applied to gain insights into oneself as well as others.

3. **Guidance**; This book provides advice and tips on how Leos can leverage their strengths, address their weaknesses and make the most of their attributes.

As you delve into the following pages we invite you on a captivating journey of self discovery and exploration through the lens of a Leo. Whether you're a Leo yourself or simply fascinated by astrology, this book aims to shed light on the path.

LEO ZODIAC SIGN OVERVIEW AND SYMBOLISM

1. **Date**; Leo, the fifth sign of the zodiac, spans from July 23rd to August 22nd.

2. **Symbol**; The symbol for Leo is the Lion. Strength, courage, and nobility represent it. Like the king or

queen of the jungle, Leos often exhibit regal qualities and hold a commanding presence.

3. **Element**; Leo is a Fire sign. Fire signs are known for their passion, energy and enthusiasm. Leos are no exception. They bring warmth and vitality to their interactions.

4. **Planet**; The ruling planet of Leo is the Sun. Leos often radiate confidence and seek to shine like the Sun in their lives.

5. **Color**; The vibrant and bold color associated with Leo is gold. This reflects Leo's love for attention and their desire to stand out.

PERSONALITY TRAITS

Leos are known for their charismatic, generous and outgoing nature. They exude a natural magnetism that draws people toward them. Some key personality traits of Leos include.

- **Confidence**: Leos have an innate self-assuredness that helps them tackle challenges head-on.
- **Creativity**: They possess a creative spirit and a flair for the drama, often enjoying the arts and entertainment.
- **Leadership**: Leos are natural leaders who can inspire and motivate others with their enthusiasm.
- **Warmth**: They have a warm and generous heart, making them loyal and protective friends or partners.

- **Optimism**: Leos tend to maintain a positive outlook on life and believe in their ability to achieve their goals.

STRENGTHS

- **Leadership**: Leos have the ability to take charge and lead with charisma.
- **Courage**: They are not afraid to take risks and stand up for what they believe in.
- **Creativity**: Leos have a strong artistic and creative streak.
- **Generosity**: They are generous with their time, affection, and resources, often willing to help those in need.

WEAKNESSES

- **Ego**: Leos can sometimes have a pronounced ego, seeking attention and validation.
- **Stubbornness**: They can be resistant to change and hold onto their viewpoints firmly.
- **Impulsivity**: Leos' fiery nature can lead to impulsive actions and decisions.
- **Dramatic**: They may have a tendency to make a big production out of small issues.

From its representation as the Lion to its association with the radiant sun, Leo holds many captivating secrets. The following chapters will explore the intricacies of Leo's personality that make them such intriguing individuals.

You will also learn all about its history through the ages, career prospects, relationships and much more.

Throughout this journey you will gain valuable insights into how Leos navigate their world and understand their compatibility with zodiac signs. Prepare to encounter stories, anecdotes and practical guidance that will deepen your appreciation for Leos in your life. Be it yourself, a loved one or a friend. This book celebrates the spirit of the leo. So let us now immerse ourselves in the captivating world of Leo where courage, creativity and charisma reign supreme!

CHAPTER 1:
HISTORY AND MYTHOLOGY

The Leo zodiac sign has intrigued humanity for generations. In this chapter we embark on a journey through the tapestry of history and mythology that envelops this sign. A deeper understanding awaits you as you become acquainted with this zodiac lion. From the earliest recorded observations to the enduring legacy of Leo in present day astrology. Here we will uncover the tales, legends and symbolism that have shaped this passionate sign. Join us as we delve into the lion hearted bravery, strength and charm associated with Leo.

HISTORICAL ORIGINS

The Leo constellation, also known as the Lion, has held a position in the night sky for generations. Its origins can be traced back to ancient civilizations, where it was observed, recorded and woven into the mythologies of diverse cultures. Here are some of the most notable accounts.

BABYLONIAN AND SUMERIAN

The ancient Babylonians and Sumerians recognized the lion figure of Leo in the night sky. They documented their observations on clay tablets dating back to the 2nd millennium BCE. Leo was associated with their narratives, often portraying it as a creature with a lion's body and eagle's wings. The Babylonians connected this constellation with the "Great Lion,". This was a being that played a role in their cosmology and religious beliefs. For them the lion has long been regarded as a symbol of protection and guidance.

ANCIENT EGYPTIAN

In Ancient Egypt the constellation Leo was linked to Sekhmet, a goddess associated with war and healing. Sekhmet was known for both destruction and healing. She was believed to have the power to bring plagues and diseases. Believers erred on the side of caution and appealed to her protective nature. As such the symbol of a lioness represented her protective nature. The Egyptians held lions in high regard. The Sphinx, a statue in Egypt with a lion's body and pharaoh's head is thought to have symbolic connections to Leo.

ANCIENT GREEK MYTHOLOGY

In Ancient Greek mythology Leo was frequently connected to the Nemean Lion. This was a creature with impenetrable skin. Hercules faced it as part of his Twelve Labors. This heroic tale became intertwined with the constellation itself, leading star maps to depict Leo as a lion. This myth highlights themes of courage, strength and heroism.

MODERN ASTROLOGY

In modern astrology there has been a shift, towards a psychological and personality based approach. While Leos still maintain their confidence and charisma, astrologers now explore their characteristics within a context of growth and self awareness. The emphasis lies on how individuals born under Leo can leverage their strengths while addressing any weaknesses. The goal is to direct them towards fulfilling lives. Although we still hold an appreciation for the symbolic aspects of Leo, modern astrology focuses on the interactive relationship between celestial forces and our individual psyches. This approach provides an introspective viewpoint, on the majestic Lion of the Zodiac.

NOTABLE EVENTS DURING THE LEO SEASON

It is important to note that astrology does not establish a cause and effect relationship with events. However certain noteworthy occurrences align with the attributes commonly associated with Leo. For instance periods of creativity, leadership or displays of courage may be more pronounced during this time.

Throughout history many influential figures have been born under the sign of Leo. While astrology does not determine one's destiny outrightly, these notable individuals possessed qualities often linked to Leos. Confidence, charisma and a strong desire to lead.

- **Napoleon Bonaparte**, born on August 15th in 1769. The French military leader and emperor renowned for his leadership and magnetic personality exemplified Leo traits. Those could be seen in his pursuit of power and his ability to inspire his troops.

- **Barack Obama**, born on August 4 1961. Obama served as the President of the United States. He was widely admired for his captivating speeches and ability to inspire millions of people. Such traits are often associated with individuals born under the Leo zodiac sign.
- **The Olympics (Creativity, Enthusiasm)**: The Summer Olympics often occur during Leo season. This global event showcases the creativity in opening ceremonies and the enthusiasm of athletes representing their countries.
- **National Independence Days (Enthusiasm, Generosity)**: Many countries celebrate their independence during this period, such as India and Pakistan. These celebrations are often marked by enthusiastic festivities and a generous spirit of unity and pride.

As we come to the end of this chapter we have delved into the stories and historical background surrounding the Leo zodiac sign. From its roots in ancient civilizations to its significant role in mythologies and beyond. Leo has always represented courage, strength and charismatic leadership.

Throughout history individuals born under the Leo sign have left their mark on the world by showcasing qualities like confidence, creativity and a natural ability to inspire others. From figures such as Napoleon Bonaparte. To transformative leaders like Barack Obama. Those with Leo personalities have truly made a lasting impact on the course of history.

The enduring influence of Leo continues to shine in astrology. While we hold the mythological interpretations, contemporary astrology provides a more comprehensive perspective on how Leo influences our lives. It guides individuals, towards self discovery, personal growth and a deeper understanding of their strengths and challenges. In an evolving world Leo's timeless attributes of self expression, vitality and unwavering determination remain relevant and highly valuable.

If you're interested in delving further into the history and mythology of Leo there are recommended sources worth exploring. These include texts, ancient writings and more contemporary works. All of which offer a wealth of knowledge and insights that will allow you to immerse yourself in the world of Leo and astrology. Whether you're seeking a perspective or a modern take, these resources provide an abundance of information to delve into and appreciate.

- **"The Astrology Encyclopedia"** by James R. Lewis: This comprehensive reference book offers insights into the history of astrology. Including the Leo sign, its symbolism, and historical significance.
- **"The Secret Language of Astrology"** by Roy Gillett: Delve into the symbolism and interpretation of Leo in modern astrology. This has a focus on personality traits and personal development.
- **"Star Myths of the Greeks and Romans"** by Theony Condos: Explore the rich tapestry of Greek and Roman mythology. Includes stories related to the Leo constellation.

- **"The Babylonian World"** edited by Gwendolyn Leick: This book provides a glimpse into the ancient Babylonian civilization. Early observations of celestial bodies and their significance took root.
- **"The Oxford Companion to World Mythology"** by David Leeming: An invaluable resource for understanding mythologies from around the world. Includes those associated with the Leo constellation.
- **"The Only Astrology Book You'll Ever Need"** by Joanna Martine Woolfolk: A modern guide to astrology that covers all aspects of the zodiac signs. Leo is included with insights into compatibility, career, and more.

CHAPTER 2: LOVE & COMPATIBILITY

This chapter explores how individuals born under Leo can navigate love and relationships with their unique qualities. Leos, the captivating zodiac sign ruled by the Sun and symbolized by the Lion, brings a fiery and passionate approach to matters of the heart. From their pursuit of passion, to their generous nature, Leos leave a lasting impression on the canvas of love. Within this chapter we explore the complexities of Leo's approach to love. We will also delve into how they connect with other zodiac signs.

Join us on a journey through Leo's love life as we examine their vibrant personalities and how they harmonize with other signs in the zodiac. Whether you're a Leo seeking a partner or someone intrigued by their heart, this chapter promises an enthralling exploration of love and compatibility.

THE LEO APPROACH TO LOVE

Leos, ruled by the Sun and symbolized by the Lion, bring their lively and theatrical personalities into their romantic relationships. Overall their approach to love is characterized by warmth and passion. Let's take a closer look at how Leos approach love.

- **Passion and Intensity**; Leo individuals are renowned for their passionate nature. When they fall in love they do so with intensity and wholeheartedness.

- **Generosity and Affection**; Leos are generous lovers who take pleasure in spoiling their partners. They thrive on making their loved ones feel adored and valued. Expect surprises, heartfelt compliments and grand gestures from a Leo partner.

- **Desire for Attention**; Leos have a need for attention and admiration. In love they often seek partners who can provide them with the praise they yearn for. This doesn't imply selfishness. Rather it reflects their longing to feel appreciated.

- **Loyalty and Devotion**; like the unwavering Lion, Leos are devoted companions. They take their commitments seriously. Trustworthiness and loyalty play a central role in Leo's approach to love.

- **Dramatic Flair**; Leos add a captivating touch to their relationships infusing them with drama and style. They take pleasure in crafting memorable moments. Their imaginative nature and love for theatrics bring a sense of thrill to the relationship.

- **Independence and Confidence**; Leos are self confident individuals. This can be both an asset and a challenge in their relationships. They value partners who admire their self assuredness while also respecting their need for space and independence.

- **Challenges**; Leos longing for attention and admiration can sometimes lead to feelings of jealousy or possessiveness if not handled well. Additionally they have a tendency to be stubborn. This might lead to conflicts when their pride is at stake.

- **Compatibility**; Leo often finds compatibility with signs that appreciate their warmth and vitality such as Aries and Sagittarius. Libra and Gemini also make good matches as they offer the communication skills and intellectual stimulation that Leos enjoy.

In summary the Leo approach to love and romance is marked by passion, generosity and a desire to make their partners feel like royalty. They infuse excitement and theatrics into their relationships creating magical experiences. While it's important to understand their need for attention and admiration, Leo's loyalty and devotion make them exceptional loving partners. Surely for those who appreciate such energy.

COMPATIBILITY WITH OTHER SIGNS

LEO AND ARIES

Leo and Aries are both Fire signs. Their relationship is often characterized by intense passion and enthusiasm. They share a zest for life and thrive on excitement. This dynamic duo can have a vibrant and energetic partnership, with both partners encouraging each other's ambitions. However, their strong personalities may occasionally clash, leading to power struggles. Communication is key to resolving conflicts. Overall when they work together, they can achieve remarkable goals.

LEO AND TAURUS

Leo, a Fire sign and Taurus, an Earth sign, have contrasting approaches to life and love. Leo seeks excitement and attention. Taurus values stability and security. Despite their differences, this combination can work well if they appreciate each other's strengths. Leo's passion can ignite Taurus's sensuality. Taurus can provide Leo with a stable foundation. However, Leo's desire for admiration may clash with Taurus's need for loyalty and commitment.

LEO AND GEMINI

Leo and Gemini share a dynamic and intellectually stimulating partnership. Both signs are social, communicative and love to have fun. Leo's charisma and Gemini's wit make them an engaging couple in social settings. However, Leo's desire for commitment and stability may clash with Gemini's need for variety and freedom. Trust and open communication are essential for this relationship to flourish.

LEO AND CANCER

Leo and Cancer have contrasting elements, with Leo as Fire and Cancer as Water. While this combination can have challenges, it can also be deeply nurturing and passionate. Leo's warmth and protective nature can complement Cancer's emotional depth and sensitivity. However, Leo's desire for attention may inadvertently hurt Cancer's feelings. Building trust and open communication is vital for long-term harmony.

LEO AND LEO

Two Leos in a relationship can create a fiery and intense connection. They share similar values, such as the desire for attention and admiration. However, their shared love for the spotlight can lead to power struggles and occasional clashes of ego. Both partners must be willing to compromise and share the spotlight for the relationship to thrive. When they do, this duo can create a passionate and dynamic partnership.

LEO AND VIRGO

Leo, a Fire sign and Virgo, an Earth sign, have contrasting approaches to life and love. Leo seeks excitement and attention. Virgo values practicality and order. This pairing may require patience and compromise, as Leo's extravagant nature may clash with Virgo's practicality. Virgo's attention to detail can help Leo in achieving their goals. Leo must appreciate Virgo's need for stability and avoid overwhelming them with drama.

LEO AND LIBRA

Leo and Libra share an affinity for beauty, socializing, and harmony. Both signs appreciate the finer things in life and enjoy a sense of style. This combination can create a loving and balanced partnership. Leo's charisma complements Libra's charm. Together they can engage in intellectual and passionate conversations. However, Leo's desire for attention may occasionally compete with Libra's need for balance and fairness. Communication and compromise are essential for a harmonious relationship.

LEO AND SCORPIO

Leo and Scorpio have passionate and intense personalities, making their relationship both magnetic and challenging. Leo's outgoing nature may initially intrigue Scorpio. However their possessiveness and jealousy can trigger Leo's desire for freedom. Trust is a significant issue in this partnership. Both partners must work on open communication and mutual respect to overcome their differences. If they can find common ground, their connection can be deeply transformative.

LEO AND SAGITTARIUS

Leo and Sagittarius share a Fire sign bond characterized by enthusiasm, adventure and a love for freedom. They have a dynamic and passionate connection, enjoying each other's company in social settings and taking on adventurous activities. Both signs value honesty and directness in communication. This can strengthen their bond. However, Leo's desire for attention may occasionally clash with Sagittarius's independent spirit. Trust and mutual respect are key to resolving any conflicts.

LEO AND CAPRICORN

Leo, a Fire sign and Capricorn, an Earth sign, have contrasting approaches to life and love. Leo seeks excitement and attention. Capricorn values structure and ambition. This pairing can be challenging, as Leo's desire for admiration may clash with Capricorn's focus on their goals. However, if they appreciate each other's strengths, Leo's charisma can complement Capricorn's ambition.

Meanwhile Capricorn's stability can provide Leo with a solid foundation.

LEO AND AQUARIUS

Leo and Aquarius have a dynamic and intellectually stimulating partnership. They both appreciate creativity and enjoy socializing, making them an engaging couple in various social circles. Leo's charisma and Aquarius's unique perspective complement each other. However, Leo's desire for attention and admiration may occasionally conflict with Aquarius's need for independence and individuality. Trust and open communication are essential for a harmonious relationship.

LEO AND PISCES

Leo and Pisces have contrasting elements, with Leo as Fire and Pisces as Water. This combination can be both passionate and challenging. Leo's charisma and Pisces's sensitivity can create a deeply emotional connection. However, Leo's desire for attention and Pisces's need for emotional security may sometimes clash. Leo must be considerate of Pisces's feelings. Pisces should appreciate Leo's warmth and protectiveness. Building trust and understanding is crucial for their relationship's success.

In a nutshell those are the main compatibilities of Leo and the other Zodiac signs. Overall one must remember in astrology that while compatibility can provide insights, individual personalities, values and communication styles play significant roles in the success of a relationship. Ultimately, every partnership is unique.

TIPS FOR DATING AND RELATIONSHIPS WITH A LEO

Dating and being in a relationship with a Leo can be an exhilarating experience. Known for their fiery, passionate, and confident nature, Leos are often seen as the life of the party and can bring a dynamic energy to any relationship. However, understanding their unique characteristics is key to building a strong, harmonious partnership. Now we'll delve into essential tips for dating and maintaining a thriving relationship with Leo. Overall, these tips will help you navigate the ups and downs of loving a Leo.

FOR MEN DATING LEO WOMEN

- **Show your appreciation**; Leo women thrive on admiration and compliments. Let her know how much you admire her qualities, accomplishments and appearance.
- **Plan exciting dates**; Leos love adventure and grand gestures. Organize thrilling and unforgettable dates that cater to her sense of fun and excitement. Surprise her with a weekend getaway or getting tickets to an exhilarating event.
- **Share the spotlight**; While Leo women enjoy being in the center of attention it's important to give them space to shine too. Show interest in their passions and achievements without overshadowing them in gatherings.
- **Be supportive**; Leo women appreciate partners who believe in their dreams and support their

ambitions. Encourage them to pursue their goals while being their cheerleader.

- **Respect their independence**; Leo women value their independence greatly. Give them the freedom they need when they require it, trusting them to handle their affairs. Avoid being overly possessive.

FOR WOMEN DATING LEO MEN

- **Offer admiration**; Leo men have a desire for admiration and recognition. Compliment his accomplishments and express appreciation for his efforts and unique qualities.
- **Engage in his passions;** Leo men often have interests or hobbies that they deeply care about. Show interest by participating in those activities, alongside him or encouraging him to pursue his endeavors.
- **Allow him to shine**; Leo men thrive on being in the spotlight. Support his need for attention. Take pride in his accomplishments. Be a partner when he receives recognition.
- **Maintain communication**; Leo men value honesty and direct communication. If any concerns or issues arise in the relationship, address them openly and respectfully.
- **Respect his pride;** Leo men can be proud individuals and their egos are sensitive. Steer clear of criticizing or belittling them as it can dent their confidence. Instead provide feedback when necessary.

As we wrap up this chapter discussing love and compatibility, for Leo it's important to highlight the valuable role astrology can play in our understanding of relationships. While exploring the characteristics of Leo and how it interacts with zodiac signs can offer insights we must remember that each person is a unique combination of traits and experiences. The dynamics of a relationship are not solely determined by the stars but by the personalities, backgrounds and life stories involved.

Astrology can be a tool for gaining perspective and igniting curiosity about how we connect with others. It encourages us to delve into the details of our personalities as well as those of our partners often leading to deeper understanding and empathy. However it should be seen as a source of inspiration rather than a rulebook.

When it comes to matters of the heart, effective communication, trust and mutual respect are principles that hold significance. These elements form the pillars of healthy relationships; they surpass astrological signs and configurations to create a foundation for enduring love and companionship.

So let astrology serve as your guide while adding an element of fascination to your journey through love and relationships. Always remember to ground your connections in timeless principles such, as understanding, compassion and respect.

By combining the insights gained from guidance with an understanding of behavior and emotional desires one can skillfully navigate the complex journey of relationships experiencing both elegance and personal satisfaction.

CHAPTER 3:
FRIENDS AND FAMILY

Leos, symbolized by the Lion and guided by the Sun, bring a unique combination of loyalty, generosity and leadership to both their friendships and families. Whether they take on the role of life's party spark, protective guardian or nurturing presence. Leo individuals play central roles in the lives of those who are most important to them. Join us as we delve into Leo's web of friendships and family where their warmth and charm radiate brightly.

LEO AS A FRIEND

When you become friends with a Leo you welcome a companion who embodies charisma, loyalty and passion into your life. The qualities of a Leo friend often reflect their warm hearted nature associated with this symbol. Here's what you can expect when you have Leo as a friend.

- **Loyalty**; Leos are loyal friends. Once they commit to a friendship they remain steadfast through thick and thin. You can rely on them for unwavering support and trust.
- **Warmth and Generosity**; Leo friends are well known for their warm nature. They enjoy showering their friends with affection, compliments and thoughtful gestures. They will make you feel truly valued and appreciated.
- **Natural Leaders;** Leos have an inclination to take charge in situations. They are often the ones organizing meetups. With a Leo friend you'll never be short of adventures and memorable experiences.
- **Positive Energy**; Leos possess enthusiasm and radiate positivity. They uplift those around them. Being in their company is often uplifting.
- **Supportive**; Leo friends are fiercely protective while also providing support. They will go to lengths to ensure that their friends are safe, happy and successful. You can trust them with your secrets knowing that they will always have your back.
- **Social Butterflies**; Leos enjoy having a big circle of friends. They can introduce you to new people

or help you expand your social network. Their outgoing nature adds liveliness and enjoyment.

- **Drama and Entertainment**; Leos have a knack for infusing excitement and entertainment into their friendships. They excel at storytelling, cracking jokes and creating unique moments.
- **Occasional Ego**; While Leo friends are generally generous individuals they may be sensitive about their egos at times. They appreciate recognition for their accomplishments and may occasionally seek validation. It's important to acknowledge their achievements with compliments.
- **Directness**; Leos appreciate friends who are straightforward, genuine and transparent. Hidden agendas or aggressive behavior is not something they prefer.

To put it simply. Having Leo as a friend is akin to having a bright star in your life. Their warmth, generosity and upbeat energy can make your friendship feel like a celebration. With a Leo friend you can anticipate a friendship brimming with laughter, escapades and cherished moments that will stay with you forever.

LEO AND FAMILY DYNAMICS

When it comes to family dynamics, Leos have a way of bringing warmth and charisma to the forefront. Represented by the Lion and ruled by the Sun, Leos are known for their protective nature. They are cherished and distinctive members of the family unit. Let's take a look at how Leo individuals contribute to family dynamics.

- **The Natural Leader**; Leos naturally gravitate towards taking on leadership roles within the family. They are often the ones who organize family gatherings, celebrations and outings.
- **Protector and Provider;** Leos see themselves as protectors and providers for their families. They take these responsibilities seriously, going above and beyond to ensure the well being and happiness of their loved ones.
- **Affection**; Leo individuals are renowned for their warmth and affectionate nature. They express love through hugs, kisses and words of admiration. In the family setting they make sure everyone feels cherished.
- **Generosity and Thoughtfulness**; Leos generously offer their time, attention and resources to those around them. They take pleasure in giving presents and unexpected surprises to their family members. Often they go the extra mile to make their loved ones feel truly special.
- **Entertaining**; As storytellers and entertainers Leos thoroughly enjoy captivating their family. With a Leo present at family gatherings, it becomes an entertaining affair.
- **Peacemakers**; With their innate leadership abilities Leos often assume the role of peacemakers, during family conflicts. Their diplomatic approach helps mediate disputes and fosters harmony within the family.

- **Supportive**; Leo family members are supporters of their loved ones dreams and aspirations. They consistently encourage their siblings, parents and children to pursue their passions in order to achieve success.

Overall Leos play a role in creating an loving atmosphere filled with celebration. Their natural ability to lead, generosity and knack for uplifting the spirits of their loved ones make them cherished members within their family circles.

CHALLENGES IN FRIENDSHIPS AND FAMILY FOR LEO

While individuals born under the Leo zodiac sign bring warmth, charm and generosity to their relationships, with friends and family. They also face challenges. Being aware of these challenges can contribute to fulfilling interactions. Here are some to be aware of.

- **Neediness**; Leos often have a need for attention and admiration. This can sometimes be challenging in friendships and family dynamics. It may lead to conflicts when they feel overlooked or not appreciated enough. It's important for Leos to understand that different people may express love and support in many ways. Open and honest communication about their needs is crucial.

- **Pride and Ego**; Leo's pride is a two edged sword. While it can motivate them to achieve greatness. It can also make them sensitive to criticism or perceived offenses. This sensitivity can result in conflicts when they feel that their pride is being threatened. Learning how to accept feedback without letting ego hinder relationships is vital.

- **Overwhelming Energy**; Leo individuals' boundless energy and enthusiasm may at times overwhelm others. They might come across as dominant or excessively enthusiastic causing others to feel overshadowed or exhausted. Leos should keep in mind the importance of finding a balance between their energy levels and those of their loved ones.

- **Being Considerate;** Leos may come across as self centered or overly focused on their needs and desires. This can pose challenges for others who might feel overlooked or overshadowed. It's important for Leos to actively listen to their friends and family members whilst showing interest in their lives and concerns.

- **Impulsiveness**; Leos passion and spontaneity can occasionally lead them to make impulsive decisions. This may sometimes result in misunderstandings or unintended consequences within their relationships. Taking a moment to pause, reflect and consider the potential impact of their actions can help Leo individuals make the right choices.

- **Sharing the Spotlight**; Multiple strong personalities within family dynamics might make it challenging to strike a balance when it comes to receiving attention or recognition. It's crucial for Leo to acknowledge and appreciate others by sharing the spotlight.

- **Protectiveness**; In family dynamics Leo's protective nature can sometimes lead them towards being overly protective. This might not be well received by family members. Especially if they feel suffocated or controlled. Leo individuals should strive to strike a balance, between nurturing their loved ones and giving them the freedom to make their choices.

- **Conflict Resolution**; Sometimes Leos desire to maintain harmony can lead them to avoid conversations or sweep problems under the rug. However it's important for Leo individuals to learn communication and conflict resolution skills in order to address such issues.

To summarize, Leo individuals are known for their charm, warmth and generosity. However they may also face challenges related to their need for attention, ego and strong personalities. Overcoming these challenges requires self awareness, communication and a willingness to adapt to the needs of others. With patience and understanding Leo individuals can cultivate more fulfilling relationships.

As we wrap up this chapter it's important to acknowledge that like any relationships those involving Leos require nurturing, understanding and effort to thrive. By understanding the significance of balance, humility and effective communication Leos can continue to radiate warmth, love and appreciation.

CHAPTER 4:
CAREER AND MONEY

Leos, governed by the powerful Sun and represented by the majestic Lion are propelled by a deep desire to leave their mark on the world. Within this chapter we delve into the domain of Leo's financial mindset as well as the strategies they employ to achieve success in their careers. Furthermore this chapter also provides insights on how Leo individuals can leverage their strengths along with wisdom. Ultimately this will lead them to flourish in their careers while turning their monetary aspirations into reality.

Join us as we navigate through the maze of Leos career preferences, leadership qualities and creative pursuits. Discover how their natural charm and unwavering determination propel them towards their dreams.

CAREER PREFERENCES AND PROFESSIONAL GOALS

Leo individuals are widely recognized for their charm and self assured nature. These traits greatly influence their career choices and aspirations. Let's delve deeper into an examination of what careers Leos tend to prefer and what they aspire to achieve

- **Leadership**; Leos possess an inclination towards leadership roles. They thrive when entrusted with authority and responsibility. Whether it be managing teams, spearheading projects or taking charge of organizations. Guiding others toward success is a driving force for them.
- **Creativity**; A considerable number of Leos possess a creative streak. They gravitate towards careers in the arts, entertainment and creative industries. Here they can express their talents freely. Acting music, theater, fashion design and visual arts provide platforms for them to showcase their skills while reveling in the limelight.
- **Public Speaking and Communication**; With great communication skills and an eloquent demeanor Leos have a talent for public speaking. They excel in roles that involve addressing

audiences. As such they seek to inspire change with their words.

- **Entrepreneurship**; Leos embody an entrepreneurial spirit. They find pleasure in the freedom and creative opportunities that come with being an entrepreneur. As such they often have visions for their own ventures.
- **Education and Training**; Leo individuals are attracted to roles that involve teaching and mentoring. They have a passion for sharing their knowledge and expertise with others whether it be as educators, coaches or trainers. They take pride in helping others learn and develop.
- **Event Planning and Management**; Leos possess a talent for organizing and hosting events. Careers in event planning and management allow them to utilize their skills while indulging in their love for creating experiences for others.

- **Healthcare and Healing**; Some Leos are drawn to healthcare careers. Particularly those focused on healing and holistic wellness. They may pursue professions as doctors, therapists or counselors where their empathy and compassion can truly shine.
- **Philanthropy**; Leos have caring hearts always aspiring to make a positive impact on the world around them. They may find themselves gravitating towards careers in philanthropy or areas where they can contribute to meaningful causes.

KEY STRENGTHS

Leo individuals possess a charisma and self assurance that sets them apart as leaders. Their natural leadership skills shine through due to their confidence and ability to make choices. This is why they excel when placed in leadership roles.

Here are some more strengths that propel them forwards.

- **Charismatic Personality and Strong Presence**; Leos possess a charm and presence that captivates those around them. In work environments this charisma aids them in building connections, negotiating effectively and leaving a memorable impact.
- **Confidence and Self Assurance**; Leos radiate self confidence, which is an asset in the workplace. Their belief in their abilities

encourages them to take on challenges and make good decisions.

- **Communication Skills**; Communication is one of Leo's main strengths. They excel at conveying ideas whether through speaking engagements, presentations or interpersonal interactions. Their eloquence and clarity make them excellent communicators.

- **Motivating Teams;** Leos have a talent for motivating and inspiring their colleagues. They can elevate team morale, encourage productivity and foster a sense of unity among team members leading to performance levels.

- **Creativity and Innovation**; Many Leos possess an inclination towards creativity. They bring perspectives and innovative ideas to the table contributing to problem solving processes and the development of solutions, within their workplaces.

- **Determination and Perseverance**; Once Leos set their sights on a goal they pursue it with unwavering determination. Their persistence aids them in overcoming obstacles along the way as they strive to achieve their objectives.

In a nutshell people born under the sign of Leo bring a mix of leadership qualities, charm, self assurance and innovation to the workplace. Their talent, for motivating others, communication skills and ability to inspire make them natural leaders and valuable team members. Leo's optimistic outlook, perseverance and flexibility empower them to thrive in positions. Overall this makes them highly valued assets for any organization lucky enough to welcome them.

CHALLENGES AND STRATEGIES TO OVERCOME THEM

As we have seen, Leo individuals possess a set of qualities that contribute to their professional success. Their strong personalities, although beneficial, can sometimes pose challenges. It's crucial for Leos to strike a balance between seeking attention and maintaining humility while also navigating office politics with tact.

While individuals born under the sign of Leo possess strengths that contribute to their lives they may also encounter specific hurdles related to their personalities and career aspirations. By recognizing and addressing these challenges head on, Leo individuals can navigate their career paths effectively. Here are some common obstacles faced by Leo individuals along, with strategies to overcome them;

Desire for Recognition

- Challenge; Leos often crave recognition and appreciation. When they feel undervalued or overlooked it can negatively impact their motivation and job satisfaction.
- Strategy; To combat this challenge Leos should actively seek feedback and acknowledgment for their contributions. They should proactively communicate their achievements to supervisors and colleagues. This will ensure that their accomplishments receive recognition.

Additionally focusing on motivation and finding fulfillment in growth can be beneficial.

Managing Ego

- Challenge; Leo individuals may struggle with managing their pride and ego which can lead to conflicts with colleagues or superiors.
- Strategy; To overcome this challenge Leos should practice humility and remain open minded. Actively listen to others perspectives. Being receptive to opinions can help them keep their egos in check. Seeking feedback and constructive criticism will also assist in maintaining a balanced perspective.

Balancing Leadership and Collaboration

- Challenge; Leos thrive in leadership roles. But they may face challenges when required to collaborate or work in team positions.
- Strategy; It's important for them to actively seek opportunities to work in teams. There they can listen to others' ideas and recognize the value of team efforts. Through learning how to be a team player while maintaining their leadership qualities, they can contribute to a harmonious work environment.

Taking things personally

- Challenge; Leo individuals might take criticism personally due to their egos, which can impede their professional growth.

- Strategy; To tackle this challenge Leos can develop resilience by reframing criticism as an opportunity for improvement. They should focus on feedback and leverage it to refine themselves.

Spontaneous

- Challenge; Leo's passion and spontaneity can sometimes lead them towards decisions that may not always be in their interest.

- Strategy; In order to address this challenge Leos should practice calculated decision making. Taking a step back to evaluate options and seeking input from others before making decisions is a wise move. Furthermore, creating a decision making process that includes reflection and analysis will help them avoid wrong choices.

Balance between work and personal life

- Challenge; Sometimes Leo's strong commitment to their careers can lead to an imbalance between their work and personal life. This may impact their well being and relationships.

- Strategy; To maintain a work life balance Leos should prioritize setting boundaries and making time for relaxation. It is important for them to communicate these boundaries with colleagues and supervisors while seeking support from loved ones.

Adaptability

- Challenge; Leos might face difficulties when it comes to adapting to changes or setbacks in their lives.
- Strategy; To overcome this challenge Leos can develop adaptability skills by embracing change as an opportunity for growth. They should focus on problem solving, resilience and learning from challenges rather than perceiving them as failures.

In conclusion individuals with Leo traits possess confident personalities and strong, self assurance that can pave the way for success in their careers. Natural leaders, innovators and valued team members. Indeed they face challenges too. But by being self aware and employing strategies to tackle these challenges they can leverage their strengths, overcome obstacles and make a positive impact in their chosen fields. Always remember that success and financial stability are within your reach when guided by your valiant spirit and unwavering confidence in your abilities.

CHAPTER 5: SELF-IMPROVEMENT

In the world of astrology Leos are known for their confident and charismatic nature. This chapter takes us into the heart of Leo's quest for personal growth and development. We'll delve into how they can nurture their leadership skills, foster their creativity and master the art of self awareness. Inside you will discover insights into Leo individuals unique path as they strive to accomplish their goals cultivate growth and live life with unwavering vitality and purpose.

Represented by the Lion and guided by the Sun, Leos possess an unwavering determination to excel, inspire others and make a lasting impression. This chapter explores the qualities, strengths and areas where Leo individuals can grow to be their best. It delves into how they tap into their potential for self improvement and the strategies they employ to become the best versions of themselves. Join us as we embark on a captivating exploration of Leo's journey towards self improvement.

PERSONAL GROWTH AND DEVELOPMENT

Leos possess personalities filled with confidence which naturally drives them towards personal growth and development. They are motivated to achieve greatness while leaving a lasting impact on the world. Here are some important areas and strategies that can contribute to their overall growth and development.

- **Self Reflection**; Take time to reflect on your goals, values and aspirations. It's essential to understand what truly inspires and motivates you. Developing self awareness is the first step towards growth.
- **Setting Ambitious Goals**; Leos thrive when they set goals for themselves. Define inspiring objectives for both your professional and personal life. Break goals down into manageable steps and milestones.
- **Embracing Challenges**; Don't shy away from challenges or setbacks. See them as opportunities for growth and learning. Your resilience and determination will help you overcome obstacles along the way.
- **Developing Leadership Skills**; Leverage your natural leadership qualities to foster growth. Seek out opportunities to lead whether it be in your workplace, community or personal projects.

These experiences will enhance your skills and boost your confidence.

- **Refining Communication Skills**; Continuously work on improving your communication skills. Effective communication is crucial in forming connections with others whether it's in relationships or professional settings.
- **Expanding Knowledge**; Engage in learning by pursuing education, attending workshops or engaging in self study activities. Expanding your knowledge base will significantly enhance your development.
- **Balancing Confidence with Humility**; While confidence is valuable it's equally important to maintain a sense of humility. Be receptive to feedback and be willing to acknowledge when you don't have all the answers.
- **Find mentors**; Seek guidance from individuals you admire and respect. Mentors can offer insights, advice and support as you navigate both your professional and personal journey.
- **Gratitude**; Cultivate a sense of gratitude for the blessings in your life. Appreciate the people, opportunities and experiences that have contributed to your growth and achievements. Gratitude is a solid foundation.
- **Balance ego;** Maintain a level of self esteem and confidence while embracing humility. A balanced ego can motivate you to reach your goals and serve as an inspiration to others.
- **Celebrate**; Take time to celebrate your accomplishments no matter how big or small they may be. Acknowledge your achievements and

milestones as you progress on the path of self development.

- **Openness**; Stay open minded towards change, be adaptable to experiences and different perspectives. This openness can lead to growth and a broader understanding of the world around us.

- **Networking**; Continue building connections in social spheres. Networking can provide opportunities for personal development and learning.

- **Wellness**; Make it a priority to take care of your well being. Prioritize activity, a well rounded diet and adequate rest. Ensure you have the energy levels for pursuing your ambitions. For Leos specifically it can be beneficial to explore creative outlets for expression. For example art or music as this can contribute to growth and fulfillment.

In summary the journey of growth and self development for Leo individuals involves leveraging their strengths while remaining open to learning and embracing challenges. By setting goals, honing leadership skills and striking a balance between confidence and humility Leos can continue to evolve. Ultimately they can leave a lasting legacy of growth and achievement on the world stage.

LEVERAGING STRENGTHS AND OVERCOMING WEAKNESSES

Just like individuals of any zodiac sign Leos possess a unique set of strengths and weaknesses. It is important to understand and make the most of these qualities in order to experience growth and achieve success. Here's a guide that outlines how Leo individuals can effectively utilize their strengths while working on their weaknesses.

STRENGTHS

- **Leadership**; The innate leadership qualities that Leos possess are truly assets. To harness this strength actively seek out leadership roles or projects where you can confidently lead and inspire others.
- **Confidence**; Embrace your confidence. Remember to avoid arrogance. Utilize your confidence to tackle challenges head on and step out of your comfort zone in order to achieve professional growth.
- **Communication Skills**; Your ability to communicate effectively is a tool. Continually work on refining your communication skills by focusing on listening and empathetic communication. This will help you to connect with others on a deeper level.
- **Charisma**; Make use of your charisma to build relationships and social networks. It has the potential to open doors and create opportunities for both personal and professional advancement.
- **Creativity**; Embrace your creative side in all aspects of life. Personal or professional. Seek avenues for expression utilizing your thinking abilities to solve problems creatively and make a positive impact.
- **Determination**; Your determination acts as a driving force behind achieving success. Set goals for yourself while maintaining focus. Also be open to adapting when necessary.

WEAKNESSES

- **Ego**; Keep in mind the importance of staying humble and avoid arrogance. While having self confidence is crucial, too much pride can hinder growth and harm relationships. Practice being humble. Remain open to feedback from others.

- **Impulsivity**; Leo individuals spontaneity may sometimes lead to bad decisions. It's beneficial to establish a decision making process that involves consideration of options, consequences, values and seeking input from others. Overall this will help you avoid bad choices.

- **Desire for Recognition**; While it's natural to desire recognition for your accomplishments it's important not to make it your sole motivation. Find motivation in the work you do. Remember that not all achievements will be immediately acknowledged. Sometimes you have to work diligently in silence.

- **Balancing Leadership and Collaboration**; Learn how to strike a balance between showcasing your leadership skills while also fostering teamwork. Recognize when it's appropriate for you to take the lead and when it's better to empower others so they can shine.

- **Handling Criticism**; Cultivate resilience in the face of criticism. Seek feedback from others and use it as a tool for improvement.

- **Work Life Balance**; Aim for an equilibrium between work commitments and personal life. Don't let your career aspirations overshadow your relationships or well being. Set aside time for relaxation, hobbies and spending quality moments with family.

- **Patience**; Develop patience within yourself by allowing time required to accomplish your goals. Rushing into things can often result in stress or mistakes. Take your time and ensure accuracy, even if it means slowing down.

Remember to lead a fulfilling life it's crucial to embrace your strengths and work on your weaknesses. Utilize your strengths to achieve greatness while dedicating yourself and persevering through addressing your weaknesses. Overall this balance will contribute to a satisfying life.

The potential for growth and self improvement is limitless. In the case of Leos, they possess the potential to become great leaders, innovative creators and empathetic communicators. Their journey towards self improvement is a pursuit of excellence fueled by their enthusiasm for life and unwavering belief in their abilities.

As they navigate the path of self improvement, Leo individuals can leverage their strengths, address their weaknesses and shape a life filled with purpose, vitality and infinite success. The road ahead is illuminated by their ambition. Guided by the sun and lion that constantly propels them towards new realms of personal growth and accomplishment.

CHAPTER 6:
THE YEAR AHEAD

This chapter serves as your guide to navigating the currents that will shape your life over the year ahead. As a Leo your personality and unwavering confidence are beautifully complemented by the energy of the Sun and the Lion, which govern your astrological sign. This chapter warmly invites you to delve into the events that will influence aspects of your life. Love, career, finances, health, personal growth and self discovery in the year ahead.

Throughout this chapter we will explore movements, eclipses and celestial alignments with your Leo spirit on your journey through life. By gaining an understanding of how these cosmic forces interact with you as a Leo individual you will be empowered to make wise decisions, seize exciting opportunities and overcome challenges with grace and determination.

The upcoming year presents itself as a canvas upon which you can paint your ambitions, dreams and aspirations. So come along with us as we embark on this voyage uncovering celestial guidance that will inspire you to radiate brightly while pursuing your passions and charting a fulfilling path, towards a future filled with brilliance.

HOROSCOPE GUIDE FOR THE YEAR AHEAD

Welcome, Leo individuals, to a year brimming with opportunities, challenges and personal growth. As the mighty Lion of the zodiac, you're known for your charisma, leadership and boundless ambition. In the year ahead, your unique qualities will shine brightly as you navigate the cosmic currents. Here's a horoscope guide to help you make the most of the year ahead.

CAREER AND FINANCES

This year, your career ambitions will take center stage. Leverage your leadership skills to seize new opportunities for growth and advancement. Be open to collaboration and teamwork. Partnerships may bring exciting projects your way.

Stay adaptable and embrace change, as it could lead to unexpected career breakthroughs.

Your financial prospects look promising this year. Your determination and creativity can lead to financial gains. Consider long-term financial planning and investments to secure your future. Be cautious about impulsive spending and ensure your financial decisions align with your long term goals.

Leo individuals' career paths and financial situations will be influenced by the celestial movements of the year. Here are some key astrological events to watch for in relation to your professional and financial endeavors.

- **Saturn in Aquarius (All year)**: Saturn's influence in Aquarius encourages discipline and hard work.

It may require Leo individuals to establish a solid foundation for their career goals and financial stability.

- **Uranus in Taurus (All year)**: Uranus in Taurus can bring unexpected changes in your financial situation. Be prepared to adapt to new financial opportunities or challenges.
- **Mars in Leo (July 17 to August 31)**: Mars in your sign boosts your career drive. It's a favorable time for taking on leadership roles, pursuing promotions, or launching new projects.
- **Jupiter in Pisces (December 28, 2023 to December 20)**: Jupiter's transit can bring fortunate circumstances in your career and financial pursuits. Be open to new opportunities and partnerships.
- **Mercury Retrogrades (Multiple times throughout the year)**: Be cautious during Mercury retrogrades. They may affect communication in your workplace and financial transactions. Double-check details and avoid signing important contracts during these periods.

LOVE AND RELATIONSHIPS

In your relationships, your natural charm will draw people closer to you. Nurture your relationships by actively listening to your loved ones. Be mindful of your ego. Practice humility to maintain harmonious relationships. In matters of the heart, your charisma will be a magnet for potential partners. Existing relationships may deepen as you invest time and effort into nurturing them. Keep your heart open to new romantic experiences and connections.

Family bonds will be essential sources of support and comfort. Consider making improvements to your home environment to enhance your sense of security and well-being.

For Leo individuals, matters of the heart will be significantly influenced by the astrological events of the year. Astrology offers insights into the ebb and flow of relationships and the potential for love to flourish or face challenges. Here are some key astrological aspects to consider.

- **Venus Retrograde (December 19, 2023 to January 29)**: This retrograde period may prompt Leo individuals to reevaluate their values in relationships. It's a time for introspection and refining what they seek in love and partnership.
- **Venus in Leo (June 6 to July 3)**: During this period, Leo's charisma and magnetism will be amplified. It's an excellent time for romance and rekindling the flames of passion in existing relationships.
- **Mars in Leo (July 17 to August 31):** Mars in your sign brings heightened passion and assertiveness. It can fuel both romantic pursuits and conflicts. Use this energy wisely to communicate your desires and needs.
- **Jupiter in Pisces (December 28, 2023, to December 20)**: Jupiter's transit can bring expansion and growth in your relationships. Be open to new experiences and opportunities for personal and romantic growth.
- **Eclipses in Leo-Aquarius Axis (Throughout the year)**: Lunar eclipses in Leo and Aquarius

may bring shifts in your love life and partnerships. These eclipses can herald significant changes or revelations in your relationships.

HEALTH AND WELLNESS

Prioritize your physical health with regular exercise and a balanced diet. Practice stress management techniques to maintain your vitality. Pay attention to your mental health and seek support if needed. Remember, seeking help is a sign of strength.

Leo individuals' health and wellness are closely connected to astrological influences. Pay attention to celestial events that may impact your well-being and consider the following advice.

- **Solar Eclipse in Leo (April):** This powerful event can mark a period of personal transformation. Use it as an opportunity to set intentions for improved health and vitality.

- **Lunar Eclipses in Leo-Aquarius Axis (Throughout the year):** These eclipses may bring emotional intensity. Practice self-care, engage in stress-reduction techniques, and maintain a balanced lifestyle.

- **Jupiter in Pisces (December 28, 2023, to December 20):** Jupiter's transit can enhance your overall well-being. Explore holistic health practices and consider incorporating spirituality into your wellness routine.

PERSONAL GROWTH AND SELF-DISCOVERY

This year offers ample opportunities for personal growth and self-discovery. Set ambitious personal goals and work on developing your self-awareness. Embrace your creative side and seek outlets for artistic expression.

Travel may be on the horizon, offering you fresh perspectives and exciting experiences. Embrace opportunities for adventure and exploration. Whether it's a new destination or a novel endeavor.

Explore your spiritual side and seek inner peace through meditation, mindfulness, or spiritual practices that resonate with you. Trust your intuition and inner guidance to navigate life's challenges.

Astrological events can be powerful catalysts for personal growth and self-discovery. Here's how Leo individuals can make the most of the year ahead.

- **Lunar Eclipses in Leo-Aquarius Axis (Throughout the year)**: These eclipses may prompt self-reflection and transformation. Embrace change and be open to new perspectives.
- **Venus in Leo (June 6 to July 3):** During this period, focus on self-love and self-expression. Explore your creative side and take time for personal passions.
- **Jupiter in Pisces (December)**: This transit offers opportunities for spiritual growth and inner exploration. Consider meditation, mindfulness, or spiritual practices to facilitate self-discovery.
- **Mars in Leo (July 17 to August 31):** Use this period to assert your individuality and take bold steps toward personal goals.
- **Saturn in Aquarius (All year)**: Saturn's influence encourages self-discipline and self-improvement. Set clear intentions for personal growth and work diligently toward your aspirations.

By staying aware of these events and considering how they may impact us, Leo individuals can approach the year with purpose, resilience and commitment.

Overall this year offers you the chance to shine brighter than ever before. Embrace your natural strengths, stay open to growth, and take bold steps toward your goals. Your magnetic energy and determination will lead you to success and fulfillment.

As the Sun governs your sign, remember that you carry its radiant energy within you. Embrace the opportunities, face the challenges with confidence and bask in the warmth of your own brilliance throughout the year ahead.

KEY ASTROLOGICAL EVENTS AND THEIR IMPACT ON LEO:

Astrological events play a significant role in shaping the experiences and energies that Leo individuals encounter throughout the year. As a Leo, your Sun sign is ruled by the Sun itself, making you particularly attuned to the celestial movements and their influence on your life. Here are some key astrological events and their potential impact on Leo individuals.

- **Solar Eclipse in Leo;** When a solar eclipse occurs in Leo, it can be an incredibly powerful and transformative time for you. It may usher in new beginnings and opportunities for self-discovery. Use this period to set ambitious goals, as the energy of a solar eclipse can amplify your intentions and desires.

- **Mercury Retrograde;** Mercury retrogrades can affect communication and decision-making, and as a Leo, you might feel the impact in your interactions with others. Be mindful of miscommunications and delays, and use this time to review and reflect on your plans and goals.

- **Venus in Leo;** When Venus, the planet of love and beauty, moves through Leo, it enhances your charisma and attractiveness. This period is favorable for romance and enhancing your personal style and self-expression.

- **Mars in Leo;** When Mars, the planet of action and motivation, transits Leo, your drive and determination are amplified. This can be a time of increased energy and assertiveness, making it an excellent period to pursue your goals with passion and vigor.

- **Full Moon in Leo;** A Full Moon in your sign can bring heightened emotions and a sense of culmination. It's an ideal time to reflect on your achievements, express yourself creatively, and release anything that no longer serves your growth.

- **Jupiter Transits;** Jupiter's transits through various signs can impact your opportunities for expansion and growth. Pay attention to Jupiter's movements, as they can bring fortunate circumstances and new adventures into your life.

- **Saturn Transits;** Saturn's transits may bring challenges and lessons, but they also offer opportunities for discipline and long-term growth. Use Saturn's influence to work diligently toward your goals and build a strong foundation for your ambitions.

- **Lunar Eclipses;** Lunar eclipses can trigger significant emotional shifts and changes in your personal life. Be prepared for moments of insight and transformation during these celestial events.

- **New Moon in Leo;** New Moons are potent for setting intentions and initiating new projects. Take advantage of the New Moon in Leo to plant the seeds of your dreams and aspirations.

- **Outer Planet Transits;** Pay attention to the movements of outer planets like Uranus, Neptune, and Pluto, as they bring deeper and long-lasting transformations. These transits can impact your generational influences and encourage profound personal growth.

As we wrap up this chapter it's important to keep in mind that cosmic forces serve as guides in our journey. Remember that astrology offers insights and guidance. Ultimately your free will and choices play a significant role in how you navigate these celestial events. Use your Leo strengths of confidence and determination to harness the energies of the cosmos. Adapt to challenges and embrace opportunities for growth and self-expression throughout the year.

Again remember that you are in control of shaping your destiny while considering the celestial bodies as supportive companions, on this journey. As you embark on the journey in the year ahead may your way be illuminated by the brilliance of your aspirations and the warmth of your compassionate nature. May you leave behind a lasting heritage of bravery, originality and unwavering confidence.

CHAPTER 7:
FAMOUS "LEO" PERSONALITIES

Welcome to the captivating realm of "Famous Leo Personalities." In this chapter we embark on an exploration of some famous individuals born under the Zodiac sign of Leo. As we delve into the lives of these personalities you will learn how their nature, ambition and self assurance as Leos have propelled them to achieve greatness in various domains. Be it entertainment, sports, politics or entrepreneurship. Their stories are a testament to the qualities that define Leo individuals and their ability to make an impact on the world.

Join us on this journey as we commemorate the accomplishments, influence and enduring legacies of these Leo personalities whose brilliance continues to shine brightly as the Sun itself.

NAPOLEON BONAPARTE

- Date of Birth: August 15, 1769.
- Brief Biography: Napoléon Bonaparte was a French military leader and emperor. He rose to prominence during the French Revolution. He is famous for his military conquests and the Napoleonic Code. This laid the foundation for modern civil law.

- Leo Traits: Charismatic, ambitious and confident.
- Impact: Napoléon's legacy is marked by his impact on European history through his military campaigns and political reforms.
- Personal Life: He married Josephine de Beauharnais but divorced her to marry Marie Louise of Austria.

WHITNEY HOUSTON

- Date of Birth: August 9, 1963.
- Brief Biography: Whitney Houston was an American singer, actress and model. She is one of the best-selling music artists in history, known for her powerful vocals and iconic songs like "I Will Always Love You."
- Leo Traits: Charismatic, confident and creative.
- Impact: Houston's music and talent left an indelible mark on the music industry and continues to inspire artists worldwide.
- Personal Life: She had a tumultuous personal life and tragically passed away in 2012.

BARACK OBAMA

- Date of Birth: August 4, 1961.
- Brief Biography: Barack Obama is an American politician who served as the 44th President of the United States. He is known for his charismatic leadership and historic presidency.
- Leo Traits: Charismatic, confident and visionary.

- Impact: Obama's presidency marked a significant era in American politics, with accomplishments like the Affordable Care Act and the killing of Osama bin Laden.
- Personal Life: He is married to Michelle Obama. Together they have two daughters.

COCO CHANEL

- Date of Birth: August 19, 1883.
- Brief Biography: Coco Chanel was a French fashion designer and businesswoman. She revolutionized women's fashion with her iconic designs, including the little black dress and Chanel No. 5 perfume.
- Leo Traits: Confident, creative and independent.
- Impact: Chanel's influence on fashion and her enduring brand have made her a fashion icon.
- Personal Life: She had several love affairs but never married.

MARCUS GARVEY

- Date of Birth: August 17, 1887.
- Brief Biography: Marcus Garvey was a Jamaican political activist and leader of the Pan-Africanism movement. He advocated for the unity and empowerment of people of African descent.
- Leo Traits: Charismatic, confident and visionary.
- Impact: Garvey's ideas and activism laid the groundwork for the civil rights and Black liberation movements.
- Personal Life: He was married to Amy Ashwood Garvey.

MADONNA

- Date of Birth: August 16, 1958.
- Brief Biography: Madonna is an American singer, actress, and businesswoman. She is often referred to as the "Queen of Pop" and has had a profound influence on music and culture.
- Leo Traits: Charismatic, confident and creative.
- Impact: Madonna's music, style, and boundary-pushing artistry have made her a pop culture icon.
- Personal Life: She has been married twice and has several children.

ARNOLD SCHWARZENEGGER

- Date of Birth: July 30, 1947.
- Brief Biography: Arnold Schwarzenegger is an Austrian-American actor, bodybuilder, and

politician. He is famous for his roles in "The Terminator" series, bodybuilding career and his tenure as Governor of California.

- Leo Traits: Charismatic, confident and ambitious.
- Impact: Schwarzenegger's career in bodybuilding, entertainment and politics has made him a global figure.
- Personal Life: He was married to Maria Shriver and has several children.

USAIN BOLT

- Date of Birth: August 21, 1986.
- Brief Biography: Usain Bolt is a Jamaican sprinter and widely regarded as the fastest man in the world. He holds numerous records in sprinting events.
- Leo Traits: Confident, competitive and energetic.
- Impact: Bolt's dominance in track and field has made him a legendary figure in sports.
- Personal Life: Bolt has a daughter. He has been involved in various charity work.

DUA LIPA

- Date of Birth: August 22, 1995.
- Brief Biography: Dua Lipa is an English singer and songwriter known for hits like "New Rules" and "Levitating." She has won several awards for her music.
- Leo Traits: Charismatic, confident and creative.

- Impact: Dua Lipa has emerged as a prominent pop artist with a global fanbase.
- Personal Life: She is in a relationship with Anwar Hadid.

TOM BRADY

- Date of Birth: August 3, 1977.
- Brief Biography: Tom Brady is an American football quarterback known for his exceptional career with the New England Patriots and later with the Tampa Bay Buccaneers.
- Leo Traits: Charismatic, competitive and determined.
- Impact: Brady is considered one of the greatest quarterbacks in NFL history, with numerous Super Bowl victories.
- Personal Life: He is married to supermodel Gisele Bündchen and has children with her.

J.K. ROWLING

- Date of Birth: July 31, 1965.
- Brief Biography: J.K. Rowling is a British author best known for creating the beloved "Harry Potter" series, which has become a global phenomenon.
- Leo Traits: Creative, imaginative and confident.
- Impact: Rowling's books have inspired a generation of readers and made her one of the world's wealthiest authors.
- Personal Life: She is known for her philanthropic work and advocacy for various causes.

KYLIE JENNER

- Date of Birth: August 10, 1997.
- Brief Biography: Kylie Jenner is an American media personality, businesswoman, and socialite. She is known for her cosmetics company, Kylie Cosmetics.
- Leo Traits: Confident, entrepreneurial and influential.
- Impact: Jenner has built a successful business empire and is one of the youngest billionaires globally.
- Personal Life: She has a daughter and is part of the Kardashian-Jenner family.

In the world of astrology individuals born under the Leo zodiac sign shine like stars captivating others with their charm, ambition and creativity. These extraordinary individuals, such as the commanding presence of Napoléon Bonaparte, the mesmerizing melodies of Whitney Houston and the indomitable spirit of Coco Chanel serve as reminders that Leos are destined for greatness. Their influence spans many fields including entertainment, politics, sports and entrepreneurship. These have left a positive impact on history.

As we celebrate their accomplishments and legacies as Leos it is important to recognize both the effect of their astrological sign and their charismatic nature. Leos possess confidence, in abundance and an unwavering determination that continuously inspires us all. Their stories demonstrate firsthand how self expression, ambition and leadership are qualities deeply rooted in this zodiac sign. They serve as beacons of inspiration urging us to embrace our attributes while allowing our inner light to radiate like the Sun itself.

In the story of existence the captivating presence of Leo personalities remains at the forefront leaving behind a lasting legacy that shines brightly as the stars, in the night sky. As we say goodbye to this chapter, may you find inspiration in the individuals who embody the essence of Leo. Finally may you embrace your Leo characteristics to radiate brilliantly in your own personal journey.

CONCLUSION

Here we stand at the edge of discovery and contemplation. We have reached the conclusion of our journey exploring the Leo, Zodiac sign. Now we aim to distill the essence of the Leo zodiac sign bringing together the threads that have woven a tapestry of insights, revelations and inspirations.

Throughout this book we have delved into the core qualities that make Leo truly remarkable. We have celebrated Leo's charm, boundless confidence and captivating presence. Traits that distinguish Leos as born leaders and show stoppers. The innate creativity and ability to express oneself have been recurring themes in relation to Leo. These remind us of how important it's to embrace our talents and allow our inner artists to shine.

The unwavering determination and ambitious nature of individuals born under Leo have demonstrated the power of setting bold goals and pursuing them with unmatched passion. We explored Leo's passionate approach to love as their ability to create captivating connections, with partners, friends and family members.

Leo's drive for success and commitment to excellence motivates us to utilize our abilities and climb the ladder of accomplishment. We have witnessed how Leos can turn challenges into chances, for growth and self exploration emphasizing the significance of self reflection and understanding. We have explored the vastness of the universe studying how celestial occurrences and planetary forces impact individuals born under the sign of Leo.

In our journey we have covered an exploration of Leo in some enthralling chapters. Here let us summarize them for you in a concise rememender.

- **Chapter 1: History and Mythology**; In this chapter, we embarked on a journey through time to uncover the historical and mythological origins of the Leo constellation. We explored how different civilizations perceived and represented Leo in their star maps. From ancient Egypt's reverence for the lioness-headed goddess Sekhmet to Greek mythology's depiction of the Nemean Lion. Ultimately we learned how Leo has left an indelible mark on human history and imagination.

- **Chapter 2: Love & Compatibility**; Chapter 2 delved into the world of Leo's approach to love and romance. We explored the personality traits, strengths, and weaknesses of Leo individuals in matters of the heart. Compatibility with other zodiac signs was examined. From which valuable insights into potential relationships for Leos were found. From passionate connections with Aries to the harmonious partnership with Libra. Overall we unraveled the complexities of Leo's love life.

- **Chapter 3: Friends and Family**; In Chapter 3, we turned our focus to Leo's interactions with friends and family. We explored the dynamic Leo brings to friendships. Their loyalty and how they navigate relationships within their inner circles was a noticeable tenet. We also delved into Leo's role within the family unit, examining their strengths and potential challenges in maintaining familial bonds.

- **Chapter 4: Career and Money**; Chapter 4 explored Leo's career preferences and professional aspirations. We identified the strengths that make Leo individuals excel in the workplace, as well as the challenges they may face and strategies to overcome them. Leo's approach to financial matters and money management was also analyzed, providing valuable insights for achieving financial success.

- **Chapter 5: Self-Improvement**; Chapter 5 focused on personal growth and development for Leo individuals. We examined how Leos can harness their strengths and overcome weaknesses to facilitate self-improvement. The chapter also featured exercises and strategies for self-reflection, empowerment and embracing their full potential.

- **Chapter 6: The Year Ahead**; In this chapter, we ventured into the astrological realm to explore the impact of celestial events on Leo individuals in the year ahead. From love and relationships to career and wellness, we offered guidance on how Leos can navigate the cosmic energies. In turn to make the most of the opportunities and challenges that arise in the upcoming year.

- **Chapter 7: Famous "Leo" Personalities**; Our final chapter celebrated the legacies of famous individuals born under the Leo sign. We profiled iconic figures such as Napoléon Bonaparte, Whitney Houston, Tom Brady and others. There we highlighted their Leo traits, impact on history and personal lives. These Leo personalities served as inspirational examples of the power and potential of this zodiac sign.

Throughout the course of this book we have embarked on a captivating journey diving into the world of astrology. Our main focus has been, on the charismatic Leo zodiac sign. Not only have we unravel the mysteries surrounding Leo. We have also provided a comprehensive understanding of what it truly means to be an individual born under this sign. Our commitment to shedding light on the nature of Leo has been fulfilled through our exploration. An exploration of many aspects such as Leo's historical background, distinctive personality traits, relationships, career ambitions, self improvement, astrological insights and even how famous individuals embodying this sign have left their mark on the world.

The main idea we hope readers take away from this book is the notion that they are special and extraordinary individuals. The key lies in embracing your Leo essence and harnessing your strengths while confidently navigating any challenges that may arise along your path. We urge you to acknowledge and embrace your Leo traits as these qualities serve as your superpowers that can lead to growth, meaningful connections and success in life.

Astrology goes beyond being a mere belief system; it serves as a tool for self discovery and comprehension. Leo, with its characteristics, epitomizes individuality and self expression. It teaches us that each one of us is like a shining star in our way capable of leaving a lasting legacy.

To all those who fall under the Leo sign we encourage you to let your inner light shine brightly. Your charm, ambition and creativity are your gifts. Embrace your strengths, celebrate your passions and know that you possess the power to accomplish your dreams while inspiring others along the way.

To conclude let us appreciate the fascinating world of Leo and astrology. May the insights we have gained from this exploration inspire you to embark on a journey of self discovery, empowerment and unlocking your potential. Always remember that, like the Sun at the center of our system, you are a radiant force in the universe and your presence brings brightness to the world.

As we say goodbye to this book, about Leo let us carry with us the wisdom gained from embracing their Lions den. Let's embrace our Leo regardless of our zodiac sign and embody their confidence, creativity and determination.

In conclusion, always remember that while the stars above guide us it is ultimately our light that illuminates our path. May your exploration of the Leo constellation bring you inspiration. May your radiance match that of the Sun, for you are also a celestial presence, in the vast fabric of the cosmos.

www.ingramcontent.com/pod-product-compliance
Lightning Source LLC
Chambersburg PA
CBHW050602160726
48003CB00003B/1017